Life

Life. Elizabeth Arnold. Flood Editions, Chicago.

Published by Flood Editions
www.floodeditions.com
ISBN 978-0-9838893-8-0
Design and composition by Quemadura
Printed on acid-free, recycled paper
in the United States of America
This book was made possible in part through
a grant from the Illinois Arts Council

Right Whales Off Race Point / 1

    ★

Ruin / 5
The Sun / 7
A Large Sadness / 8
Sound's What Counts / 10
The Natural History of the Soul / 12
The Sun (2) / 14
Looking at Maps / 15
Earth / 16

    ★

At Brú na Bóinne / 19
Fontana dei Quattro Fiumi / 21
What Is a Person / 22
Like Water Flowing / 23

    ★

Flow Dynamics / 45
Reflection / 47
Contingency / 49
The Sparrowhawk Sits / 50
Heart Valve / 51

Trees / 53
A Woman in West Florida / 55
Osiris in Pieces / 56
Allegory / 58
DDT / 59
Campo San Barnaba / 62

★

The Mountain / 65

★

Going / 87
Life / 88
Gone / 91
The Sun (3) / 93
Hope / 94
Evidence / 97
There Is An / 99
Tomb of the Diver / 101
Feeder Stream / 102

★

The Hoopoe / 107

Acknowledgments / 111

The river groaned with thousands
Of corpses—Xanthus couldn't reach the sea.

Virgil

Life

Right Whales Off Race Point

blacker than black
and out of that

density

a spray
more like vapor

or air, a kind of rain

but going up,
or the clouds

rain comes from,

weightless, gray—
just before the flukes

that then send

all of it into the lightless
back down.

Ruin

The house a
skeleton, the flesh

rotting on the bone.

One breath
exhaled, my last.

As when the

earthquake hit
freakishly last summer.

I stood upstairs,

the house swaying
on the rolling land.

I ran outside.

The neighbors
in the street

knew what it was. I

didn't, looked
as is my nature up

for the cloud

above the trees.
But there was no

horizon to be sure of

so as to see
evidence

of the world's ruin.

The Sun

In the paper today
two close-ups of the sun shot

ten years apart,

the older one
complete with the familiar spots,

the other, current,

almost entirely clear orange,
cartoon-character-face orange.

It's thought

any face projected on a screen
is dead.
        "What can I do?"

she said about some
chronic social wrong I'd brought up.

Nothing, said the sun.

A Large Sadness

swelling, welling
in me I see

one, want that

then another with the
passing

draw

to a one more like
the first pull

pulling me toward that,

glancing
off it in the bright air,

sparkling leaves

—I see
a body in it, an eclipse!

And everything then

drained,
drained necessarily

of our light.

Sound's What Counts

in beautiful green Kerala

where the people sing like birds
—they make those

sounds I mean—

and the mantras there
like birdsong, no sense,

passed down generation to generation

as they're
taught to the monks

with an impossible exactitude,

translation being in this case
transliteration

so as to get into the air

here and in other places all over India
and the world

words of the god, the actual

sounds it is believed
a living entity let out and in an

instant made the world.

The Natural History
of the Soul

The song thrush hops, runs, stands,
the guidebook says, with its

head to one side listening for worms.

Just as the lion knew to follow St. Jerome
calmly as they

walked through the priests

who are running for their lives in
Carpaccio's painting in Venice,

birds opening their beaks

hoping to touch St. Francis, lover of views,
especially the one visible from his

home high in Assisi

until natural beauty failed him altogether
once he'd almost died

which turned him

utterly exclusively to concentrate on what can happen
mind-to-mind

—body-to-body if you're lucky!

Barring that
the steam-choked blind sky.

The Sun (2)

What if the sun gets caught, can't make it through to day, *can't make day?*

Looking at Maps

If they'd had writing in time, Cuba could have been Crete,
watery source of the Minoans and thus the Greeks.

What's lost? A possible us
growing like new foliage out of stony ground, emerging?

Last voice, first, a whole world calling—
awful, inaudible—into the unstoppable loud (roaring!)

hurricane-force sea wind.

Earth

Earth a cinder cool to the touch
rages closest to its core

a thousand degrees hotter than was thought,
wild seas of liquid metal

flailing all around as we speak,
birthing magnetic fields that reach

as far out as the solar winds allow,
pushing at what can't be seen with their

own unseeable force,
fire meeting fire in this way—

mother of us.

★

At Brú na Bóinne

The tumulus—I thought it was a hill at first
(trees grow out of one in Sulm)—

entered into.

It was a clear day, bright, the grass
bounded by its hedgerows

too green all around and down,

the fields' squares troubled
only by the Boyne

that just about makes an island of this place

snaking through.
Sunbeams don't snake,

at least not visibly,

though five thousand years have worked at the Earth's
orbit. Still

the light goes in, into the mound

through holes one to a side that tunnel
towards each other

but don't meet, the sun arriving

on time every year
unless it's cloudy.
                    But to do what?

Wake the corpse.

Fontana dei Quattro Fiumi

His head hooded in a chaotic state of shame,

the Nile god's body
like those of the other rivers

—muscular yet flaccid, the chiseled flesh slippery as water as he

seems to be about to slide
off the rocks,

his face just visible as it's turning

outward toward the viewer in
Bernini's sculpture in the Piazza Navona in Rome,

the idea being

to represent the river's unknown source.
But even if they'd found it by that time, the Europeans,

they wouldn't have.

What Is a Person

capable of feeling
while in contact with another

—to interface that way with god?

I look at the red-tiled roofs outside,
at all the angles

facing the white-blue cloudless sky

like the creases in Bellini's angel's
silver-blue dress, Tintoretto's white one

that's practically transparent in his

Annunciazione at the San Rocco
—cloth complex as thought!

Then the bells start, flood the void.

Like Water Flowing

... in landlessness alone resides the highest truth,
shoreless, indefinite as God.

Herman Melville

FOR A

Everything had to look alive inside the tomb.
Outside everything's dead

in Saqqara,

the five-thousand-year-old mastaba tombs there
above and below ground,

the above-ground part

sometimes below—though visible today
barely, everything being the same

color of sand

whether it's blowing or not
—when blowing even the air's that color!

The only signs from the outside of

a presence of mind
are letters carved into the walls

—not Arabic so it couldn't be the wind's work

articulating wispy cirrus-cloud shapes
like what waves make on the beach sometimes.

Here as opposed to that

the carving's deep, the hieroglyphs
stamped, safe inside their ovals,

each a cartouche

for the name of a person of power
who's held fast in that.

But they're worn now, fading.

Inside though, below the angled grave shaft's opening,
the human element remains:

everything there's alive though carved,

the grave's returning spirit
requiring the appearance of life

in order to be fed

so that all kinds of fish swim in the Nile
along with crocodiles and hippos

—they could live there then—

and the hunters and fishermen chasing them,
the animals alive

even as they're being killed,

a hippo in one panel
swallowing a crocodile,

the sky thick with birds beyond belief,

herons perch on lotus buds just like now
and the trees and papyrus reeds

stand as if stocked

with fleeing mammals,
one long-tailed, a hunter hanging on as it climbs.

The art isn't stiff as I'd been taught

to see it—against, say,
that of the Greeks—

made mostly by unnamed masters

and their genius students
who are all now

buried in another area.

     ★

Your front door sealed

in new paint
—I didn't think it could be cracked

and ran.
          But your voice

deepened
later on the phone, it

opened.

You stood in your village as you spoke,
Gubba.

I stood in America.

    ★

There's a whale fall in what's desert now
southwest of Cairo

showing the last stages of
losing their land-based hind limbs

—moving *out* of that
over a period

of a hundred million years
into the environment of water.

    ★

The mango trees were blooming and the
animals slept. We walked

closer to the river.

There was a little bit of light making shadows.
You were

turning away

but I saw something other as your
voice moved like the river when it

swerves past rocks it swirled,

slammed giant thumbprint-like impressions into
nobody knows how long ago,

carving a new channel.

     ★

Except for land depressions often
hundreds of miles across

sinking the surface far below sea level

so it's closer to the aquifer
—except for such places

(which are in the very lowest parts oases)

and the Nile,
there's no life in the desert

but for lizards, desert wheatears

and the tiny but otherwise
really more kangaroo-like field mice,

the jerboas,

thousands of which descended
(while his soldiers slept)

on the edible parts of the weapons

of Sennacherib's army,
leaving them defenseless in the Sinai.

The story's told in Herodotus

and in the minute barb-wire-like
cuneiform script carved deep into a

white oblong standing stone

at the University of Chicago's
Oriental Institute.

What if the river stopped,

with scant rain to the north
—so no more groundwater

rising, reaching fresh-, saltwater springs,

the tangles of the water tables
and narrow intersecting underground streams

even farther down, no more oases?

    ★

The snake-torsoed sky-god Nut swallows the sun
every day, the red disc moving through

her black-blue night interior

that's wrapped around the four sides of the ceilings
of rock-cut tombs and smaller inner rooms

in temples all over Egypt.

Sometimes it shoots across the blue like a comet,
the sun too far away to be seen as moving

so it's repeated every hour of the night

along the spine of a plunging grave shaft
guarded by complex notings and spells

to fight the monster snake gods

swimming frothing and snapping through
the underworld

where the sun goes while we're sleeping.

Cries in the full-moon night break through,
wailings of owls and what owls hunt,

lovers' high-pitched whining falling

in accelerating contrapuntal micro-bursts.
By dawn I'm on the verge of being born.

     *

His is a kind of thinking circling
—looping, more like.

Nothing is forgotten as I'd feared,

each word dropped
into the well-deep vault

—but it takes a while to learn that. It's a

good thing to learn, to trust what
you thought you'd lost

will come back

even if it won't. You have to
live in that unknowing always.

★

Walter Ong says there's no way
to stop sound and have it

in an oral state of consciousness I
keep following falteringly

—sound existing only when it's
going out of existence.

★

Dunes sing differently

in different deserts
depending on the

size of the sand grains.

I heard
something like wind

when I pushed a handful

off the top of a tall one
in the Great Sand Sea

near Libya

and the sand kept going
longer than expected in the

manner of a thinning sheet

of plasma's self-propelled
proliferation into

wrinkles and waves

—all of this occurring
as the result of the slightest

motion of my hand.

★

Those moments
voice-to-voice

stand spinning

outside anything
true or false

outside time

I think—I never
sought revenge

you never lied.

    ★

Like the Niger, when the Nile has traveled
a third of its course

it comes to the Sudd,
an inland delta

where it loses for a time
itself

through evaporation and seepage
in a 31,000-square-mile basin

invaded by marsh grasses as it
wanders through

thousands of channels and blind offshoots.
By the time it gets out

of that tangle the river's lost
half its capacity.

          *

In a dream I flew
right off the balcony,

turned into a dove

but I didn't look to hide away then
cooing, go to the nest,

but rather

grew my hands back, moved them
over the soft tops of

the new green pine growth

—rising still it seemed
and it wasn't even spring!

*

The rust-white nocturnal desert fennec fox
extended families scooting around

some unrecognizable Mubarak-era buildings
near the Aswan airport I saw on my way home

for the last time with their outsized ears—
they can hear the underground movement of prey

so maybe even also that of waves that must
if only just a little lap at the sides of the

entirely contained subterranean prehistoric
freshwater sea, the Nubian Sandstone,

some of which fell as rain a million years ago,
reaching all the way across (possibly also

holding up?) four North African countries.

★

"It's just a place"
I said to no one,

the spectral aspect

gone, all of it
—the Nile, the desert

that abuts it—

spectacle, my
feelings for

these things, you

going
faster than the

piddling remains

of glaciers
once so grand.

★

When your five sisters came
out of the dark into the garden, you

sitting, half lying down

as you like to
on the woven palm bench

rubbing your thick-socked feet, you'd been

so sick from the flu,
their beautiful round faces bringing

a new warmth into the world

and we were
both healed,

though they hadn't come for me.

★

al-rabe'a—spring

     when the dromedaries
     give birth and there's

plenty of milk, a
paradise for nomads

al-badia—everything

in the desert:
people, the animals

and customs
that distinguish life, as vs.

khala—silence

nothing but sand
like water flowing

over itself in wisps

    ★

The river's slack today
in the windless heat,

the spigot having been

turned off apparently
at the first cataract,

the end of Egypt,

where the water usually
pulls hard-muscled through

the high-packed desert flanks

in laterally cutting
drill-like spirals,

proliferating islands

that almost clot it and the
great rocks only barely

not breaking through.

The first cataract they say
but it's the last,

the Nile flowing north

after having stalled
almost completely but the

total volume's so great

what's left's running
hard through the basalt

banks of Aswan, spreading

everywhere through
the oceans after that.

Flow Dynamics

So lightly and invisibly I hardly knew it,

river of blood descending without joy back to the heart
through the frail vein all that time

—the largest of the body!—

shredded then dissolved ("obliterated")
and there was a sudden seepage

into surrounding tissue

instead of the blood pouring out as you'd expect forever,
and a new vein formed to bypass what was gone

like a wide meander

even the smallest flood ends, and the river
goes straight from that point.

But in my case the thin-walled base-ends held

forming an anabranch, a section of a river
that diverts from the main channel,

rejoins it downstream.

Local ones can be caused by or make
small islands in the watercourse

but sometimes they flow hundreds of miles

like the Bahr el Zeraf in the south Sudan that splits from the
Bahr al Jabal of the White Nile, doesn't return

until Malakal

instead of leaving behind,
as it could have with the blood being old,

a full-fledged oxbow lake

that before too long
will blister in the sun, become

a little blue scar beside the heart.

Reflection

I said

no to you
so often, couldn't see.

Do you know how that

changed you
—divided

what you saw in me

or anything
(if you did)

from what you

said
or mostly

didn't?

And another bottle
drained,

your head

lolling off the chair's back,
the mirror's

face blacked.

Contingency

In circumstances such as this there's really only
the reasonable hope of schooling the soul.

The Sparrowhawk Sits

so still on the

high electrical wire,
later in the pin oak with its

beautiful rust-dark streaks on the breast,

late light entering
the black seep of the eye,

for what seems like

eternity. Thus can a bird like that
be so ignored

by all it will devour.

Heart Valve

They told me there'd be pain

so when I felt it,
sitting at my beat-up farm desk

that looks out glass doors

onto the browning garden—plain sparrows
bathing in the cube-shaped fountain

so violently they drain it,

the white-throats with their
wobbly two-note song

on the long way south still,

and our dogs
out like lights and almost

falling off their chairs

freed of the real-time for awhile
as time began for me

to swell, slow down, carry me out

of all this almost
to a where

about as strong a lure as love.

Trees

Trees know which way's up,
rallying

after the two blizzards

just about broke them,
their bent branches so far down

—and some did break,

there was a
snapped trunk,

our narrow maple,

trying to grow
out of the stump now

reddish, soft new leaves

but they're coming out sideways.
Still, the

branches only

bent by the snow heaps
now have stems

poking up

from the ex-sides of their
down-curved limbs.

That they know

gravity,
vertigo from the inside, feel

the heave and spin of the globe,

grow skyward
from that as if crying,

I guess isn't so surprising.

A Woman in
West Florida

put her stethoscope

on the sand near where the
beach turns into houses,

the rubbery eggs below

about to split,
just as the cardiologist put his

on my loose-skinned lids

—in case the heart
couldn't get the blood there

or enough.

Osiris in Pieces

Ruler of the dead, king of the living . . .

FOR J

According to Pausanias

the colossal statue of Memnon in Thebes
was broken in two by Cambyses

and at the present day from

head to middle
is thrown down

but the rest is seated.

The statue was said to make the sound
of a lyre string snapping at dawn

—some called it singing—

until the emperor ordered repairs
and Memnon never sang again.

Two millennia later

we broke. We'd

become too seated,
lounging around the big house in our

separate rooms, in the same room

breaking
—the pieces of us

ever to be regathered by the god?

Regathered apart in separate cities
a thousand miles between

we are reborn.

Allegory

A Byzantine relief
in an out-of-the-way chapel in Venice

shows

Virtue and Vice, Vice depicted as
a rabbit, Virtue the hawk attacking it.

Virtue the hawk!

DDT

We chased the trucks that moved so slowly

through the streets in the early evenings
with their impossibly white

white smoke spreading, boiling as it rose through the

see-through air, creamy
but not cream-colored—dead white—

and we couldn't see each other

dipping into the cloud and out, back in
the thick-enough-to-drink gas version of the chemical

ridding the South of mosquito-borne diseases in the sixties.

John Muir caught malaria fifty years before
just a couple of hundred miles to the southwest,

Cedar Key on the Gulf,

and almost died before he walked
all the way back to California,

yellow fever rampant in the Bronx in the seventeenth century

(from the slave trade) and in Philly,
thousands dying in recurrent epidemics

and in other parts of the South of course,

around the Mississippi.
Had I not breathed so deeply

running through the dense inverted shade of a smoke cloud,

I might be well enough to get the vaccine, go
where no trucks spewing poison

snake through the streets

—dirt there mostly, muddy in the rainy season—
I'd so longed to see

so as to hear the people talking back and forth,

a kind of singing as they
move resolutely through the elephant grass

or glide down the Nile just north of Jinja

in Uganda, vervet monkeys leaping tree to tree above them
speaking their alarm calls,

a different one for each threat,

slick hippos with their comically small ears
for such a dangerous animal

—territorial when in water during the day and,

like the alligators I grew up with,
when on land they easily outrun humans—

splashing around now near where the river's said to start

its long path north to the Mediterranean
—four thousand miles away!

Campo San Barnaba

Look: the palace wall's on fire—no!
It's made of water.

The Mountain

Now with more dire convulsion flings
Disploded rocks, her heart's rent strings . . .

Virgil

Land's alive. I don't mean
teeming. Breathing—Etna swells!

—as well as changing

shape, height,
filling in a bay so that the castle's stranded.

Magmatic tides rise, fall in the asthenosphere,

responding to the sun and moon,
the Earth's crust bending slightly.

Earthquakes swarm across the globe.

It's feared the
very highest subterranean tides could actually

knock Earth off its axis.

★

Something practically knocked

the whole volcano over
eight thousand years ago

and a third of it slid off the island

it consisted of at that point,
fell into the sea

and the Mediterranean overflowed.

    ★

I couldn't see my feet
on the flinty ground

as I headed for one of the

flank cones,
my hair soaked from the steam

and it was cold!

—even in August with the
wind gusting unstopped by trees.

I thought I'd die, be blown

over or trip or freeze,
the rest of my group gone.

      ★

Clouds mingling with smoke
hug the peak.

Until today I'd never seen it clear,

Etna interacting with
whatever it is that makes the weather.

      ★

And the sun was lost when a
whirlwind blew

right about the time

the pre-eruption earthquakes started,
felling much of Nicolosi

on its southeast flank. Three days later

a fissure twelve miles long and six feet wide
though of unknown depth

appeared

a mile below the summit.
Six mouths opened in a line emitting

vast columns of smoke.

    ★

The composition of this fire, stones, and cinders
is sal-ammoniac, lead, iron, brass,

and all other mettals!

Stone and glass in feldspar crystals make up
much of the ground mass.

A specimen from near Borello
was found to contain

good crystals of augite

and olivine, well-striated labradorite and
titaniferous iron ore

—or chick-pea lava.

To the presence of this substance all the opacity
of the sections of Etna lavas is due.

★

An opacity traveling
sixteen miles with a width of four,

a depth of forty feet—it was a *wall*.

In just one day
multiple flank vents opened simultaneously

in a rift or row, the mountain roaring,

riffing off its stomping
loud as John Lee Hooker!

★

One of the worst eruptions happened
in 1669, though the arced remains

of an earlier cone,

Trifoglietto—before the new one
(what's there now)

built itself up
—still shows as arms

into which the lava often safely flows.

  ★

Arms of stone
but that seem other as they

radiate heat.

  ★

Beautiful mountain, mountain of the dead
whose lithic clasts and fumaroles,

whose pyroclastic flows go

under the lava showers and phreatic bursts
—engendered by the titan Enkelados,

trapped, fighting up at rock?

No way out in any case from under
as the flank vents open only once,

choke thereafter.

    ★

Who knows how many cones are covered,
sunk into newer lava.

Who knows where a vent will open.

    ★

Right on the spot where the day before
I'd made my meal with a shepherd friend

it happened.

On my return next day he said how
after an explosion

the rocks on which we'd sat together

were blown into the air
and a mouth opened

letting out a flood of fire that

rushing down with the rapidity of water
hardly gave him time to get away. It was a

flank eruption,

more dangerous because
closer to towns, the lava rising

too fast for its feeder system,

rushing like water but up, gurgling
—you can hear it from the surface—

the emerging lava red of course

but with stones of a paler red to swim thereon
big as an ordinary table.

       *

The lava's progress slowing as it cools, as it

starts to harden, the still-fluid part
going under its own

new-made rock

that's soon to be
after a couple of hundred years

black splintery ground a tree grows out of.

    ★

The air above at the peak
acts as a lens

sharpening the more and brighter stars

for hikers, Venus emitting a light
powerful enough to

cast shadows. Then the

sun appears
whiter and more tranquil.

    ★

It's said that standing on the mountain
during an eruption

is like standing on a living being

with circulating blood, blood that could tip
the planet over.

    ★

The sun hits the peak first
so that it stays night for a while

in the towns and fields below.

As if the mountain were
the one eye, us blind.

    ★

Etna has a lot of hollow space,
dried-up feeder pipes and caves—

freshwater springs rise through the mass

of accumulated lava
supplemented by at least some

subterranean water movement,

the lightweight porous volcanic rock
sitting on the denser

non-volcanic.

So the mountain is a sponge with
plenty of water for plant growth, little runoff.

What's lost is lost mostly to the sea.

★

Towns on the mountain's slopes are
built of lava,

paving stones to churches,

little soot-colored chapels to grand cathedrals,
ancient Greek theaters with their

decorative inlay patterns

of black against white
just as the melting snow reveals

blue-black cinders near the mountain's peak

where the
main science station stood.

Nothing lasts.

★

Rock moves—*flows!*
Next thing you know it's singing

in a low harmonic tremor of

kilometers-long infrasonic waves
heard only by dogs,

the lava flowing

180 feet per minute, the heat
at a distance of 120 feet

90 degrees.

The surface toward the summit
is frequently said to be so hot as to

make even resting inconvenient.

★

Every volcano has its own voice.

Some are operatic.
Others have

no singing talent whatsoever.

★

And the planets singing as they swing through space,
the universe ringing!

★

While a number of inhabitants were watching
the progress of the lava,

the front of the stream was

suddenly blown out
by an explosion as of gunpowder

and in an instant

red-hot masses were hurled
in every direction and a cloud of vapor

enveloped everything.

Thirty-six were killed on the spot
and twenty survived

but a few hours.

    ★

The lava undermined a hill
covered with cornfields,

carried the whole thing forward

a considerable distance,
with a vineyard seen at another point

just floating by.

    ★

We can't even hear an earthquake coming,
a volcano at the start

throwing its boulders up

the endless-seeming chimney to the hole
that can be the size of a human head

—as one man learned when he

crawled down
into the crater to see—

or three miles in circumference.

★

After the tsunami buried fifteen thousand
in Catania

the water of the fountain of Arethusa

more than thirty miles south
in Siracusa

turned muddy and brackish and

the fountain of Ajo near the village of Saraceni
six hundred miles north

in Tuscany

ceased to flow altogether for
two hours

then emitted water the color of blood.

★

Lying at the convergent
plate margin

that joins the African plate

to the Eurasian, what
went and let the magma through,

the weather in the ground believed

at one time to be
air furiously seeking air.

★

I thought I'd suffocate, be left
—it was

freezing, and wet

from the blanket of steam—
up there.

★

Women hung their laundry
next to the lava as it

made its way past

the ruins of their town.
They rebuilt in the same place.

★

When the lava streams approached Catania
in 1669, the Senate

accompanied by the Bishop and all the clergy,

secular and regular,
went in procession out of the city

to Monte di Santa Sofia

with all their relics and erected an altar
in view of the burning mountain and

celebrated mass

using the exorcisms accustomed upon such
extraordinary occasions,

all which time the mountain

ceased not as before
with excessive roaring to throw up

its smoak and flames with extraordinary violence

and an abundance of great
stones thrown up.

When the lava reached the city walls it

rose to the top—sixty feet!—
then fell like a waterfall down the other side.

By spring the lava reached the sea.

    ★

They tried diverting it, built new walls.
Pappalardo of Catania took fifty men

having provided them with skins for protection from the heat

and used crowbars to make
an opening in the lava.

They pierced the solid outer crust and a rivulet

of the molten interior
immediately gushed out

flowing in the direction of Paternò

whereupon five hundred men of that town
took up arms against Pappalardo and his men,

against the lava,

which did not altogether stop for four months
and two years after it had ceased to flow

it was found to be red hot

beneath the surface, and eight years after the eruption
quantities of steam escaped

after a shower of rain.

Going

On the interstate north of Yulee
late, the streetlights gone and my headlights reaching

only an inch or two at that point

before the flash of the warm-brown deer hides,
a little group grazing

so close to the highway's edge

my breath stopped, this breathing I do,
where the road skirts Okefenokee Swamp, the yards there

of white sand kept raked to warn the rattlers off,

when out of nowhere came
the blessèd tail-lights of a semi, the red dots growing

as I close, don't know

I'm being ferried into the now now, going
without fearing I can't see.

Life

Your hand full of hours, you came to me . . .

Paul Celan

FOR E

Subject to the weather,
lovely gusts of wind and better,

the kind that bend young tree trunks down

almost to the ground,
strip off my roof tiles, the sky

open as an eye and trusting

nothing will be coming through,
a membrane riding

the wind I

walk through, watch
from behind glass doors

thinking of you

coming and going like wind by way of
many and quickly shifting moods.

When the wind lifts, leaves

silence
—into which comes something punching

through, I

flinch, veer, there is, there
isn't—it's a

borderlessness:

me, you, the
me-and-you, our bodies (though

by way of that)

—they're
gone before they go.

      ★

                        And a

drop of ink falls
into a thick-glassed glass of water . . .

      ★

                                        Who
are you, what?

I know a lot without knowing.
What is knowing? Or

not—?
          Seeing's a way

to be mistaken, I saw
something

—how a hand looks

lying on a body, a brand new
way of
          —blind.

                    Which is to
let yourself
be stupid, eyes closed.

Stupefied!

Gone

after Lorine Niedecker

Dig dig into black earth.

For the seed,
for stone.

Something

green.
Alive, or only

seeming to be living?

A greenish sprout maybe
looking weak,

the glowworm letting off its

thin green light,
or a stone light enters,

emerald or jade

—that's thought to form
only under a seabed needing

pressure to emerge,

milky like the worm
whose light comes

from inside.

                 My love was
deep

—deep as what he seemed to be at night?

Seemed lives long.
Night traveling

at the speed of light. A was

he is now
on the

Passing Years River.

The Sun (3)

The red sun rose. In my peyote vision
it was god.

Hope

And a

door slammed
then cracked open,

still moving

a little bit toward me
—not to let the chaos in

but the

air going
so slowly

from the wild sudden world of you,

or the you I thought was—
everything of what slowed down

seemed to want to

stay.
                    Just as the

valve repaired will

with its closing
more completely at every beat

make the blood flow

calmly
out of the frantic heart

and then

a hand squeezed, not gripped,
so there's another

it seems

opening, the petals
freed of the mechanical

(though floating)

movement of a
time-lapsed camera's works

—nothing forced,

never a jerked
blooming's

dying on the stem.

Evidence

2.7 billion years ago

the Earth spun
faster and the Moon

was closer, the

Sun weaker, no
animals or plants back then,

the air being

not breathable.
Rain tumbling onto the ash

dug out depressions

—we only see
the imprints today

because the

top layers of rock are gone,
the thinking being

that the pits tell us

something about what
ancient air pressure was like,

pits subsequently

covered over
by further ash and

turned to stone.

There Is An

I
—and that I

am, feel

alive
in the organism

of a living world.

It isn't any proof I guess.
Who knows where this

particular brand of

I I so un-
fortunately met

comes out of or if

any of what
such a one is feeling is

feeling at all?

Only that
I can.

That's it.

A minus turning
into a plus now,

there not being

much left
anyway

reliably to be known.

Tomb of the Diver

Painted on the inside of the lid of a coffin in Paestum, he was diving into nothing all alone. To live is to die diving.

Feeder Stream

I'd climbed onto a rock

—a boulder really
I was on one side of, slipping, my boat

shooting the rapids without me.

When I looked down
I saw the water

surging then slightly going slack

and then it surged again,
the whole thing pulsing on a

slow clock, the world within

outside too—*that's* in us as the
poleward Gulf Stream's sea-water river

—at its slowest carrying

more cubic feet of
water per second than

all the world's rivers combined—

swings past Florida
loaded with whales once!

—*throbbing* as it

rides above the south-flowing
North Atlantic

Deep Water current, blood going

twenty-six yards per second.
So much of what

we know and don't, alive.

The Hoopoe

It was an accident
a few days after the mother bird,

having not that long ago flown north

across the Mediterranean,
pecked at the window every morning for a week,

one facing the other

like two portholes in my attic room,
so angrily it seemed

at the threat she saw (herself)

threatening her chicks,
one of which, grown, flew

quick as the bats darting all around the trees

and outbuildings of this
Tuscan medieval castle

the night you called from Egypt,
your voice a dim light barely getting through

the atmosphere

of the great hall the valley makes
—right through my room

Bede-sparrow-like

but in this case the long
downwardly curved-beaked hoopoe

exited the morning

with its sparkling off the vines' leaves hiding
the fragile grapes

and the olives' dull leaves even

shining!
—out of that, back into.

Acknowledgments

Versions of poems in this book first appeared in *The Account*; *Better*; *BODY*; *Forklift, Ohio*; *Gulf Coast*; *Kenyon Review*; *The Nation*; *Oversound*; *Plume*; and *Poetry*. "Heart Valve" is reprinted in *Poetry in Medicine* (Persea Books, 2014).

The epigraph to this book comes from Sarah Ruden's translation of *The Aeneid*. The epigraph to "The Mountain" comes from John Conington's translation of the same. Some sections of "The Mountain" include words and phrases from G. F. Rodwell's *Etna: A History of the Mountain and of its Eruptions* (London: Kegan Paul, 1878). The epigraph to "Life" is translated by Michael Hamburger.

My deepest thanks to Lindsay Bernal, Michael Collier, Lisa McCullough, and Stanley Plumly for their advice about the poems. Many thanks also to Amy Lowell's estate for its generous support, and to the sharp-eyed editors of Flood Editions.

Elizabeth Arnold's other books are *The Reef* (University of Chicago Press, 1999), *Civilization* (Flood Editions, 2006), and *Effacement* (Flood Editions, 2010). She is on the MFA faculty at the University of Maryland and lives in Hyattsville, Maryland.